Organized by Phoenix Art Museum
Dennita Sewell, Curator of Fashion Design

The presentation of this exhibition and
catalog is made possible by the support of
**Jonathan and Maxine Marshall and
The Marshall Fund of Arizona**

Joy Episalla
The Physical Photograph

17 February 2001–10 June 2001

**The Jonathan and Maxine Marshall
Gallery of Contemporary Art**

JoyEpisalla:
The Physical Photograph essay
© Frank Moore

JoyEpisalla:
The Physical Photograph
Phoenix Art Museum
17 February 2001–10 June 2001

Organized by Phoenix Art Museum
Dennita Sewell, Curator of Fashion Design

ISBN 0-910407-41-X (alk. paper)

Design
Mookesh Patel
Alfred C. Sanft
InfoDesign Management
Tempe, Arizona

Photography
Carrie Yamaoka
New York, New York

Additional Photography
Ken Howie Photography
Phoenix, Arizona

Lithography
Prisma Graphic Corporation
Phoenix, Arizona

Cover:

pillow #2, 1999
c-print mounted to plexiglass
triptych: 40" x 60" x .5" each

Foreword and Acknowledgments

The Phoenix Art Museum is pleased to have the opportunity to exhibit Joy Episalla: The Physical Photograph. She investigates the zone between photography and sculpture by creating large-scale photographs of everyday items presenting them as objects. This exhibition of twelve major works is the third exhibition funded by The Jonathan and Maxine Marshall Endowment. It is with their support and sponsorship that the Museum has been able to bring attention to under-recognized American artists through the exhibitions and accompanying publications. The Museum and the contemporary art world are fortunate to have friends such as the Marshalls.

Dennita Sewell, Phoenix Art Museum Fashion Design Curator, brought Ms. Episalla's work to our attention and has facilitated this exhibition. Ms. Sewell's dedication to the Museum has fostered a creative, broad approach to the role of fashion in society and art.

I would like to thank Joy Episalla for her great assistance with all aspects of this exhibition, and would also like to recognize Nick Debs and Choire Sicha of Debs & Co for their unwavering support of Ms. Episalla and her work. Mr. Frank Moore has provided a thoughtful and insightful perspective in his essay that facilitates a deeper appreciation of Episalla's work.

In closing, I would like to thank Heather Northway, Chief Registrar, Gene Koeneman, Chief Preparator, Bob Gates, Brad Pochop and Alison Van Wyck, Preparators, for organizing the shipment and installation of the exhibition. Ryan McNamara, Curatorial Assistant, supported the goals of this project, assisting with all aspects of the exhibition and catalogue development.

The goal of The Jonathan and Maxine Marshall Fund projects is to focus attention on American artists who have not gained the wide audience they deserve. I hope our visitors will agree with our selection of Joy Episalla.

James K. Ballinger
The Sybil Harrington Director
Phoenix Art Museum

Joy Episalla
The Physical Photograph

Frank Moore

The things we touch in daily life, bed pillows for example, change. They may take on a weariness of stains before we're through with them. Our rugs faithfully record the positions of furniture, the concealed passage of an extension cord beneath, the abrasions of foot traffic. There are moments when we see these things, when we "read" them. Given enough time, enough history, the domestic objects which surround us may become our biography.

These are the sort of objects Joy Episalla photographs and she imbues them with a distinctive emotional intensity. She has cited the apartment that Catherine Deneuve inhabits in Roman Polanski's *Repulsion* as an example of the unsettling effect she seeks in her work.[1] Polanski's film script contains many references to physical details: walls, a fire grate, suitcases, crumpled sheets, ceilings, doors and door handles, optical distortions on the surface of a teakettle. These familiar things take on a creepy quality accentuating the vulnerability and psychic fragility of the central character, Carol (played by Deneuve). Early in the script Polanski uses simple details to ease us into Carol's state of mind:

> "Now we see what CAROL sees, a small crack on the surface of the wall by an air vent.
>
> But the spectator cannot be certain whether it really exists or is the product of
>
> his imagination"[2]

Later in the film Carol leans against the hallway wall only to find that it has suddenly become soft and clay-like. Playing with perception is very much a part of Episalla's method as well. In a large but minimal image (cushion #3, 2000) depicting two buttons and a seam on a well worn piece of leather furniture, she has indicated that she sought to heighten the resemblance of the leather to human skin.[3] Things are never quite what they seem in Episalla's work; and, as

1 Conversation with the artist, December 2000

2 Polanski, Roman: *Three Film Scripts*. Icon Edition. Harper and Row, © Lorimer Published Ltd., 1975

3 *Naturalistic Photography for Students of the Art*, 1889. Second Edition 1890. Third Edition, revised, 1899.

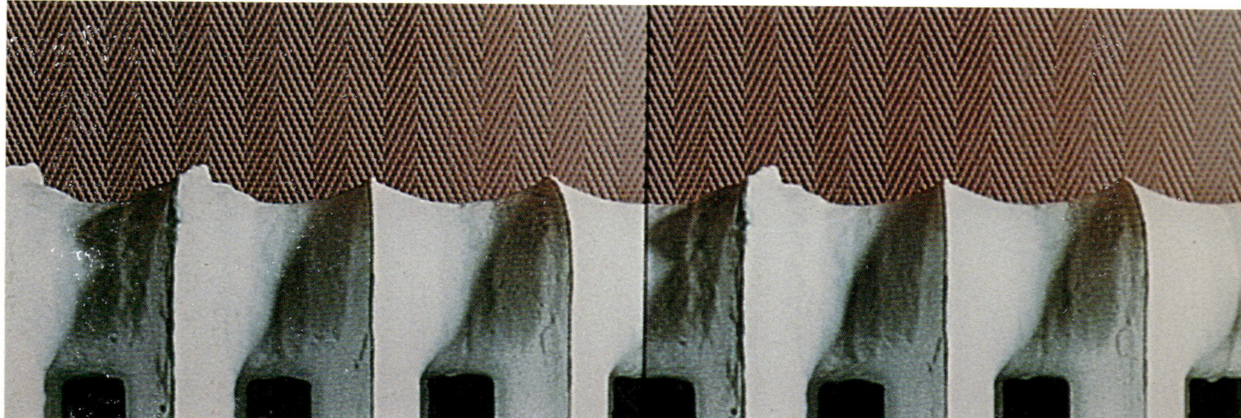

in a film, it is through the accumulation of such readings that the larger ambitions of her work emerge.

Picture this: at the far end of a room a series of six overlapping photographic images, each 26"x 39", (radiator #1, 2000), are leaning against the wall. Teeth. A giant set of aqua choppers with fibrous gums seem to bite the floor. In fact, the bottom half of each image is a section of a radiator, the upper half a mauve sisal-like woven mat. It is difficult to discern which is in front of the other: there is a near perfect confusion of figure and ground in part because the cropping of the image has removed all the visual clues. The modular form of the radiator repeats like Brancusi's endless column laid on its side. The actual juncture of floor and wall is hidden behind the leaning images, and because the teeth read like a bizarre architectural molding, the piece subtly distorts the space in the room. Up close, one can see that each image is mounted behind a 1/2 inch thick slab of Plexiglas. The piece has considerable mass. The edge of the slab diffracts the image, which glimmers and from certain angles appears to be mounted on the face of the slab. Episalla enhances this effect by cutting away a thin margin of the white plastic material backing the photographic image: the image thus appears to have no physical thickness and simply becomes fused with the object.

The physical quality of the work goes hand-in-hand with a minimal pictorial sensibility, and reflects the fact one that Episalla was formally trained as a printmaker and painted for many years. Images are usually cropped and rarely include more than one object. The compositions are frontal and geometric and often evoke references to abstract painting. Her photographs of

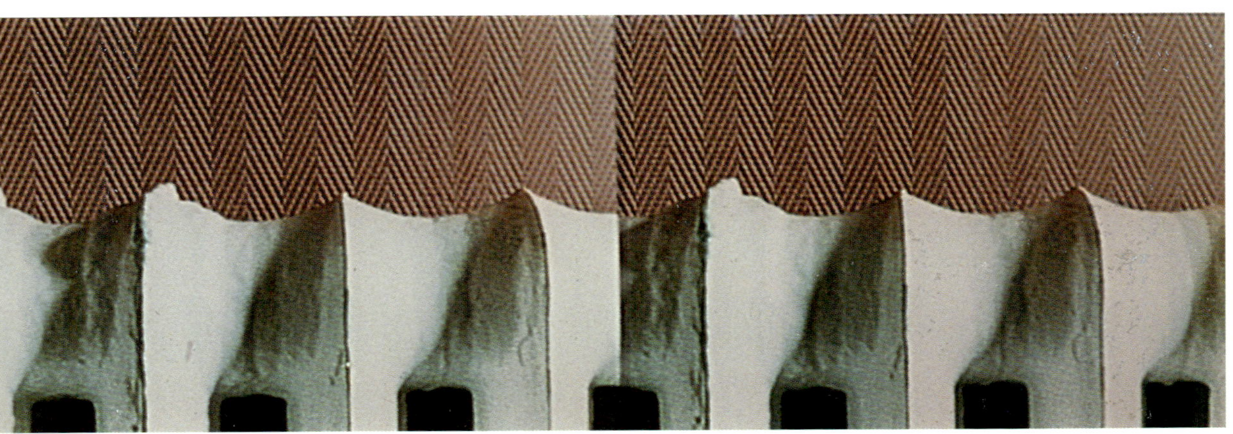

radiator #1, 2000
c-print mounted to plexiglass
5 panels: 26 x 39 x .5 inches each

striped curtains, for example, call to mind the work of Gene Davis, Kenneth Noland and Bridget Riley. But because these are, after all, photographs, there are organic events and textures that are illusionistic and sensual in a photographic sense; and Episalla manipulates hue, saturation and lightness in the darkroom to give these images an effect utterly unlike that of painting.

She shoots these images with a very high speed film, and then pushes the film to achieve a characteristic "grain" (particles of emulsion that become visible when the negative is enlarged). This grain becomes highly visible when a 35mm negative is enlarged to a final print size of 26" x 39". Seen at a distance her images often appear muted or drab in color, but one has only to approach any work closely to perceive swirling constellations of these particles of emulsion in an impossible array of colors; vibrant yellow and pink, delicate ultramarine blue and chartreuse. This effect is further enhanced by the pearly, iridescent quality of the photographic paper she uses. The shift from drab order to sparkling confetti suggests a sense of delight and freedom at the core of Episalla's work.

In appropriating the strategies of painting and incorporating them with her photographic practice, Episalla extends a venerable artistic tradition. The renowned nineteenth century photographer P.H. Emerson, the great champion of Julia Margaret Cameron, founded a school of photography that sought the same artistic freedoms enjoyed by the great painters of his day (he cites Millet and Corot for example). Like the early Impressionists, he was influenced by discoveries in optics made by scientists like Hermann von Helmholtz. He sought to free photography from a slavish obsession with evenly sharp focus throughout an image:

> "For example, the realist, if painting a tree a hundred yards off, would not strive to reder the tree as it appears to him from where he is sitting, but he would probably gather leaves of the tree and place them before him, and paint them as they looked within twelve inches of his eyes, and as the Modern Pre-Raphaelites did, he might even imitate the local color of the things themselves. Whereas the naturalist painter would care for none of these things, he would endeavor to render the impression of the tree taken as it appeared to him standing a hundred yards off, the tree taken as a whole, and as it looked, modified, as it would be by various phenomena and accidental circumstances. The naturalist's work we should call true to nature. The realist's work we should call false to nature."[4]

In his influential book, *Naturalistic Photography*, published in 1889, he proclaimed:

> "The rule in focussing, therefore, should be, focus for the principal objects in the picture, but all else must not be sharp: and even the principal object must not be as perfectly sharp as the optical lens will make it."[5]

Because of this, Emerson was roundly attacked by his contemporaries for introducing "fuzziness" to photography. He responded

> "...we have nothing whatever to do with any "fuzzy school." Fuzziness, to us means destruction of structure."

He goes on to qualify this by saying

> "We have, then nothing to do with "fuzziness," unless by the term is meant that broad and ample generalization of detail, so necessary to artistic work."

4 ibid.

5 ibid.

These words, written more than a hundred years ago, embody the same searching spirit, the same willingness to cross boundaries and subvert expectations that distinguish Joy Episalla's work today. She, like Emerson, is a disciplined rebel.

In a remarkable group of large floor pieces Episalla photographs the open maw of a variety of women's handbags. They are apparently empty and the darkness at the center of the image becomes a *trompe l'oeil* hole or fissure. They become vaginas, and may initially seem debased by their position on the floor. The fact that some of the handbags depicted are quite opulent, lined with silk or satin, may provoke tart associations. But they also evoke Mother Earth and remind one of mythological passages to the underworld, such as those undertaken by Demeter or Orpheus. Given Episalla's playfulness, it's hard not to think of Alice and the rabbit hole as well, although the voice emanating from this hole sounds more like Grace Slick than Lewis Caroll.

What is also striking about these pieces is that by displaying them on the floor Episalla is challenging the viewer to consider them as sculptures. The dimensions of a piece relative to the dimensions of the room, and its position in the space, take on the same sort of formal value that one experiences in relation to a piece by, for example, Carl Andre. Yet clearly there is a feminist and revisionist challenge being issued: these formal values are now being assigned a gender. And although a sense of vulnerable physicality is central to Episalla's work, the work is not passive. A work not included in the present exhibition, Handbag #2, has a rather sharp looking zipper which might leave the viewer feeling a bit like Carol contemplating one of those cracks.

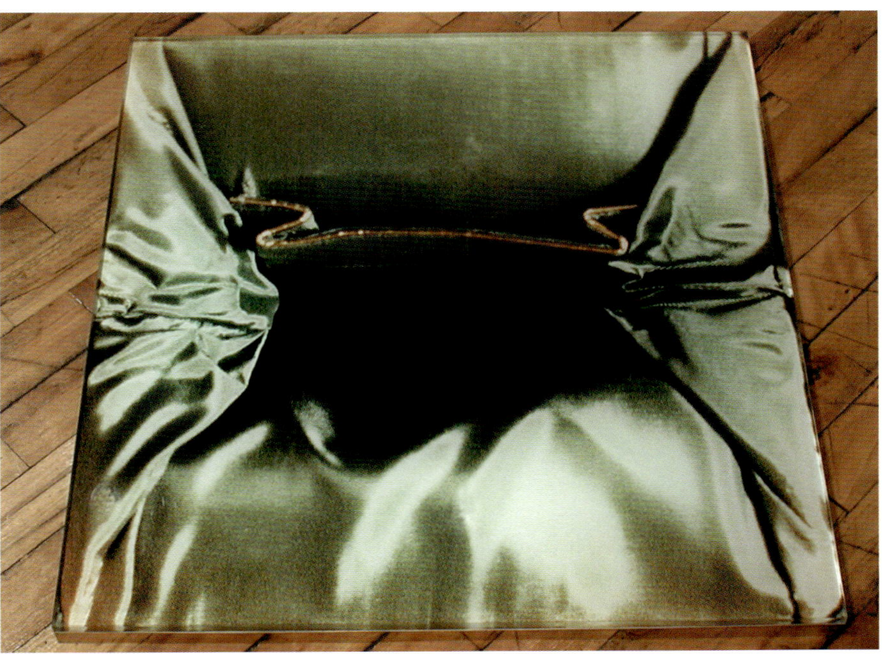

***handbag #6,* 2000**
c-print mounted to plexiglass
34 x 32 x .5 inches

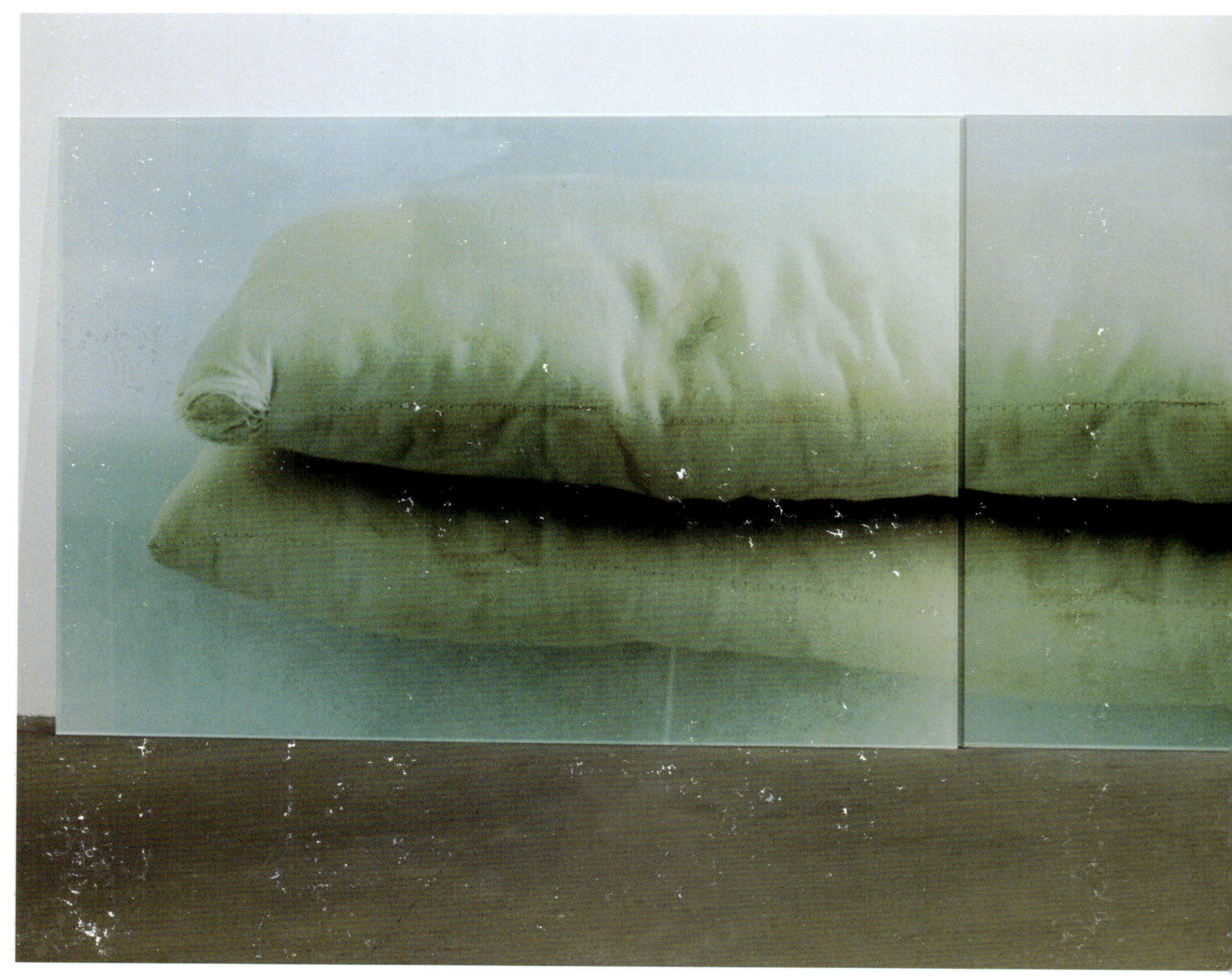

***pillow #2,* 1999**
c-print mounted to plexiglass
triptych: 40 x 60 x .5 inches each

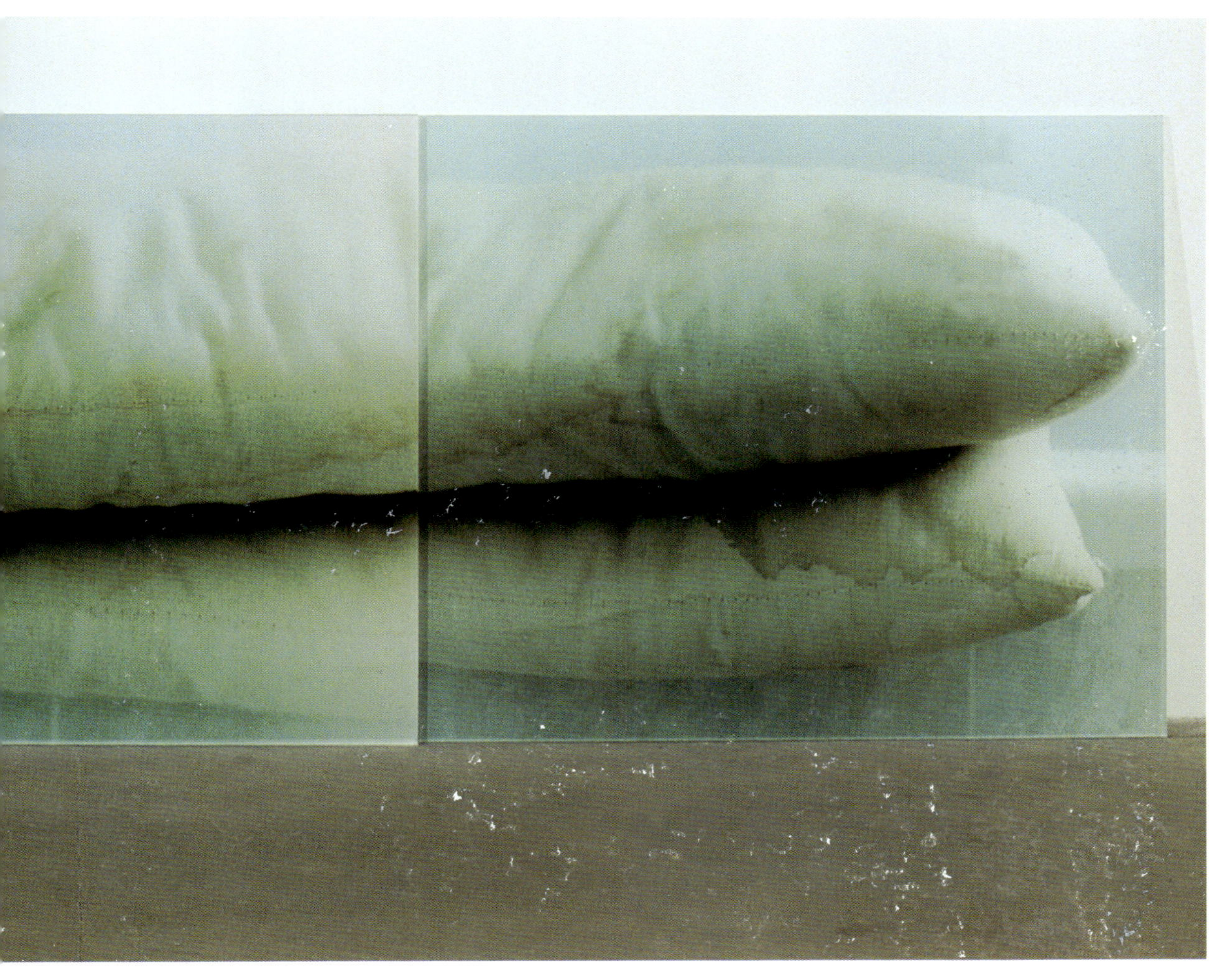

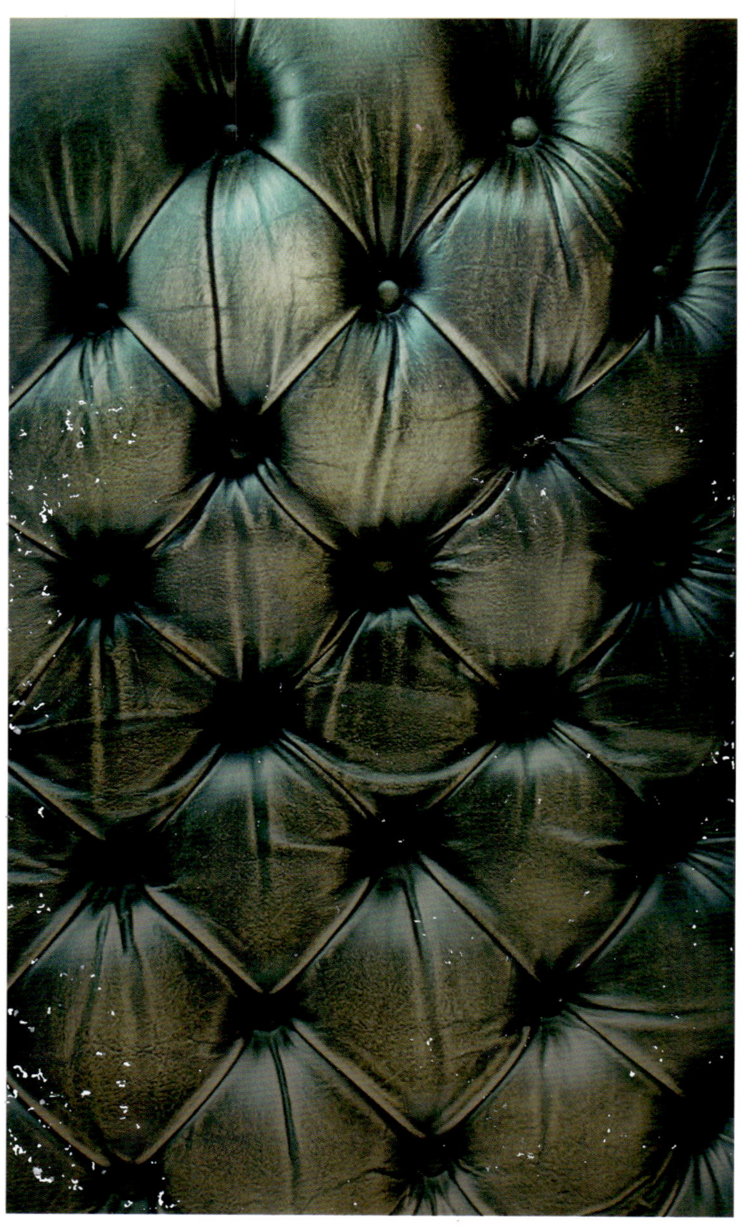

cushion #2, 2000
c-print mounted to plexiglass
66 x 40 inches

For me it's not simply about printing a negative and trying to get the right color and the right light. It's also about finding the right physical quality in that photograph to make it much more visceral. It starts to cross over the boundary of sculpture but, also, of real/unreal. It's about bringing out what those things feel like-what the emphasis is. Trying to figure out its strongest point.

– Joy Episalla

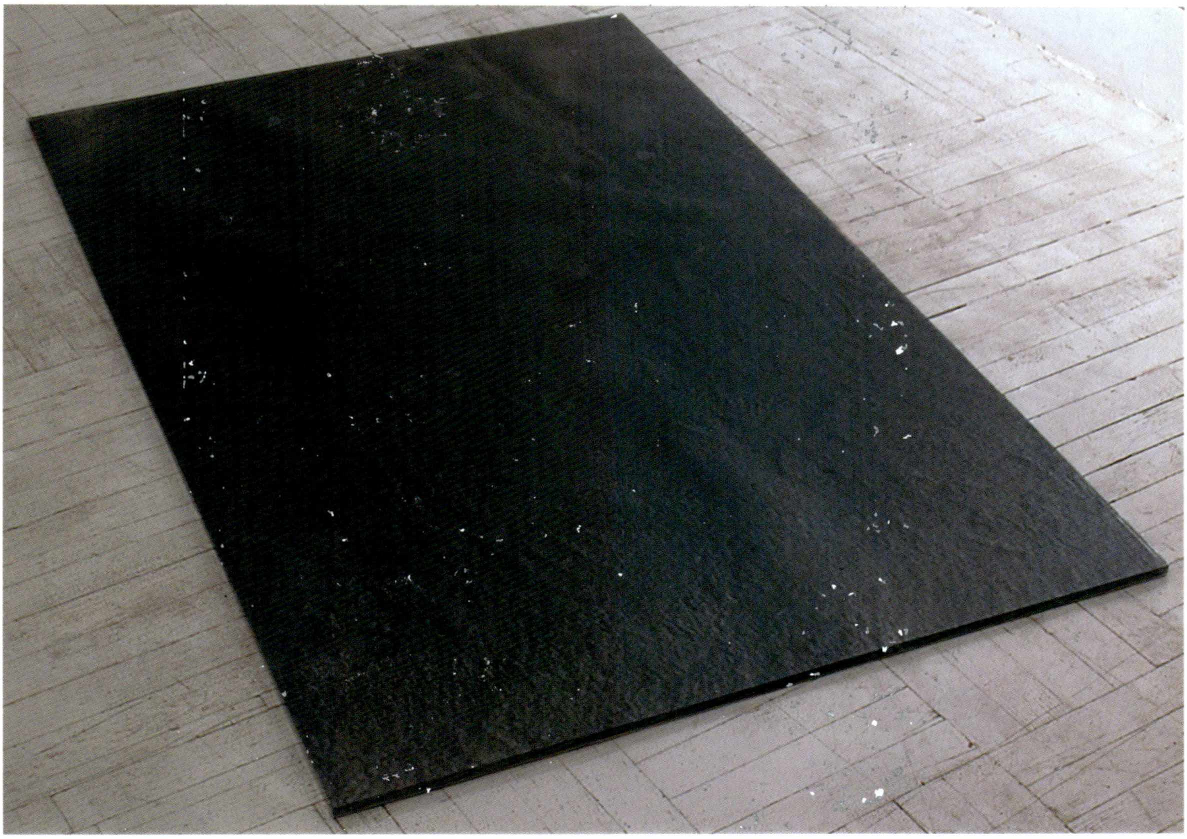

carpet #5, 2000
c-print mounted to plexiglass
36.5 x 58.5 x .5 inches

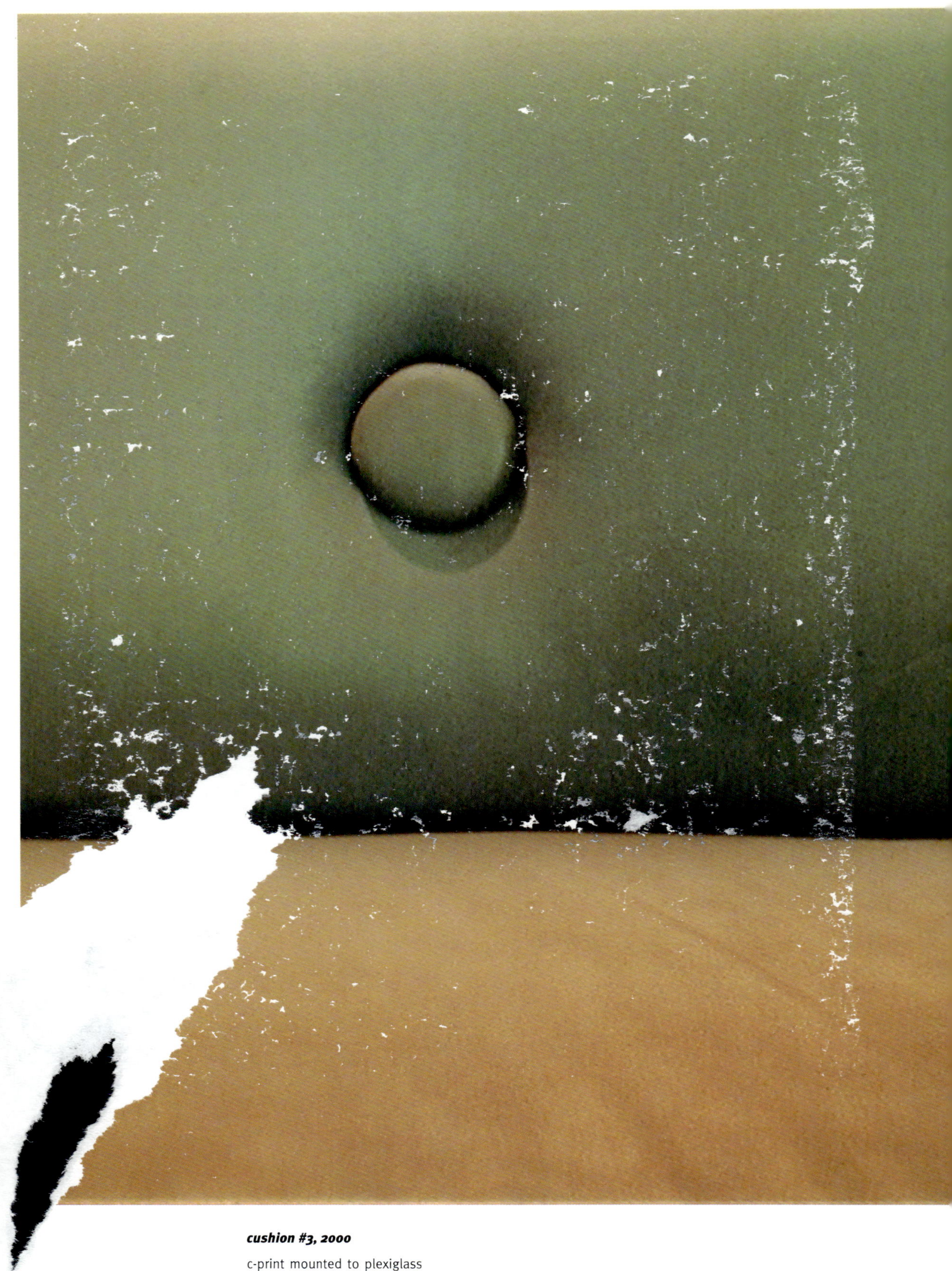

cushion #3, 2000
c-print mounted to plexiglass
60 x 40 x .5 inches

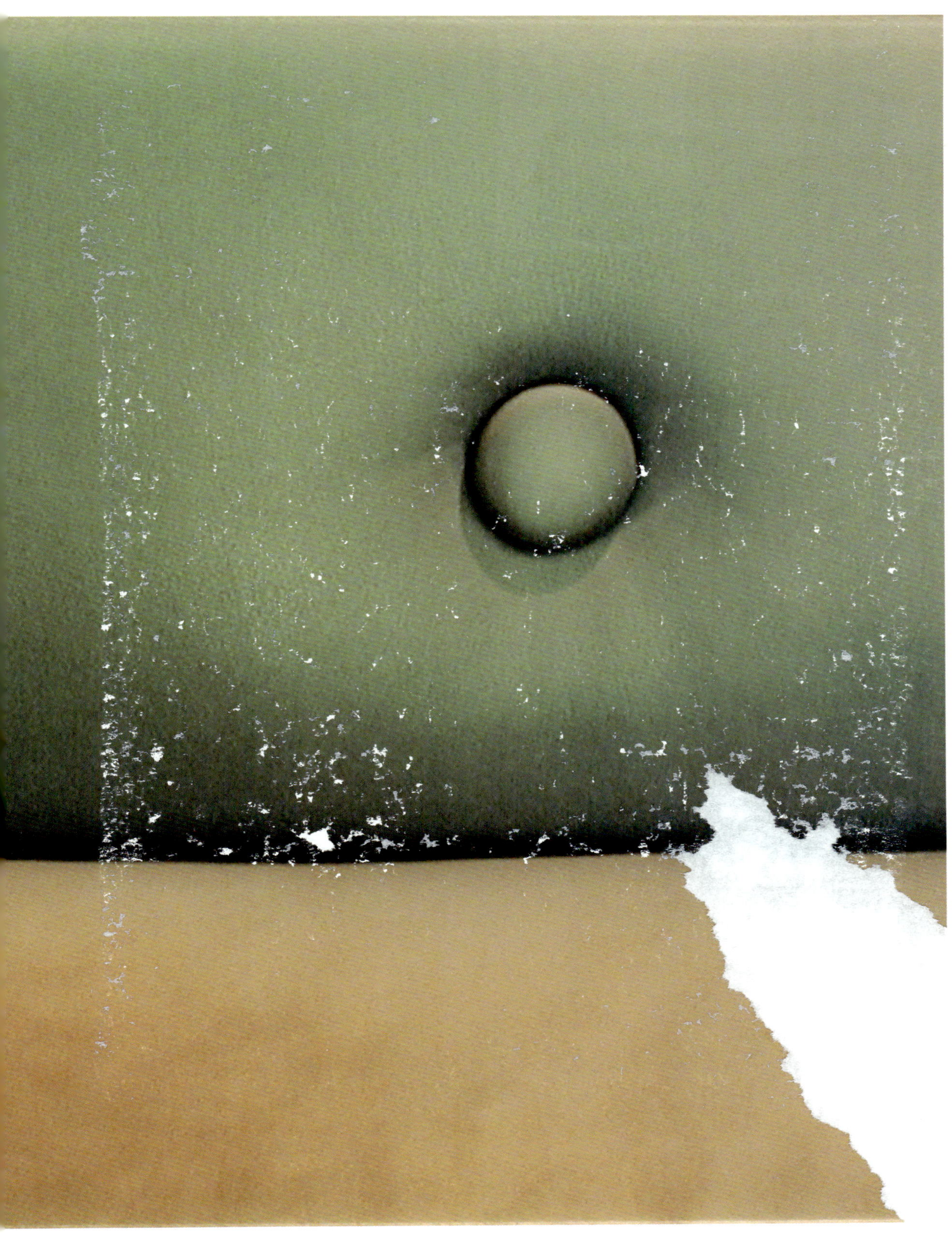

carpet #3, 1999
c-print mounted to plexiglass
40 x 30 inches

It was a really cool day. There
was an ugly beige carpet;
all of the furniture had been
removed from the room and
there had been a lot of traffic.
There were stains and
impressions left from where
the furniture had been and
footprints. I just thought:
There is the whole world here.
It has so much information.
That's fascinating. The human
presence which is absent.

– Joy Episalla

__curtain #26,__ __2000__
c-print mounted to plexiglass
40 x 30 inches

carpet #1, 1999
c-print mounted to plexiglass,
40 x 30 inches

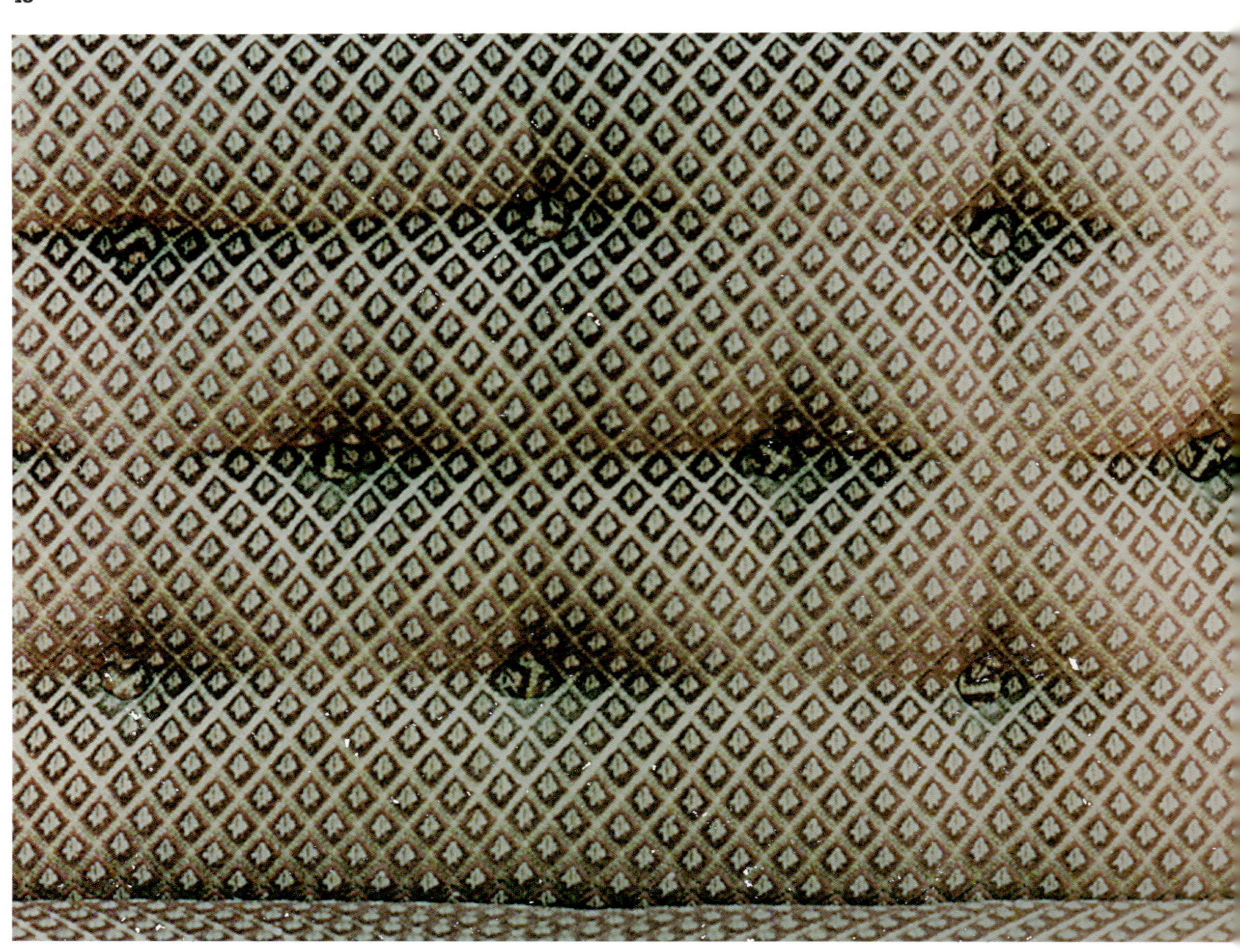

One panel doesn't do what two of them do. The
get a much longer, almost snake-like, almos

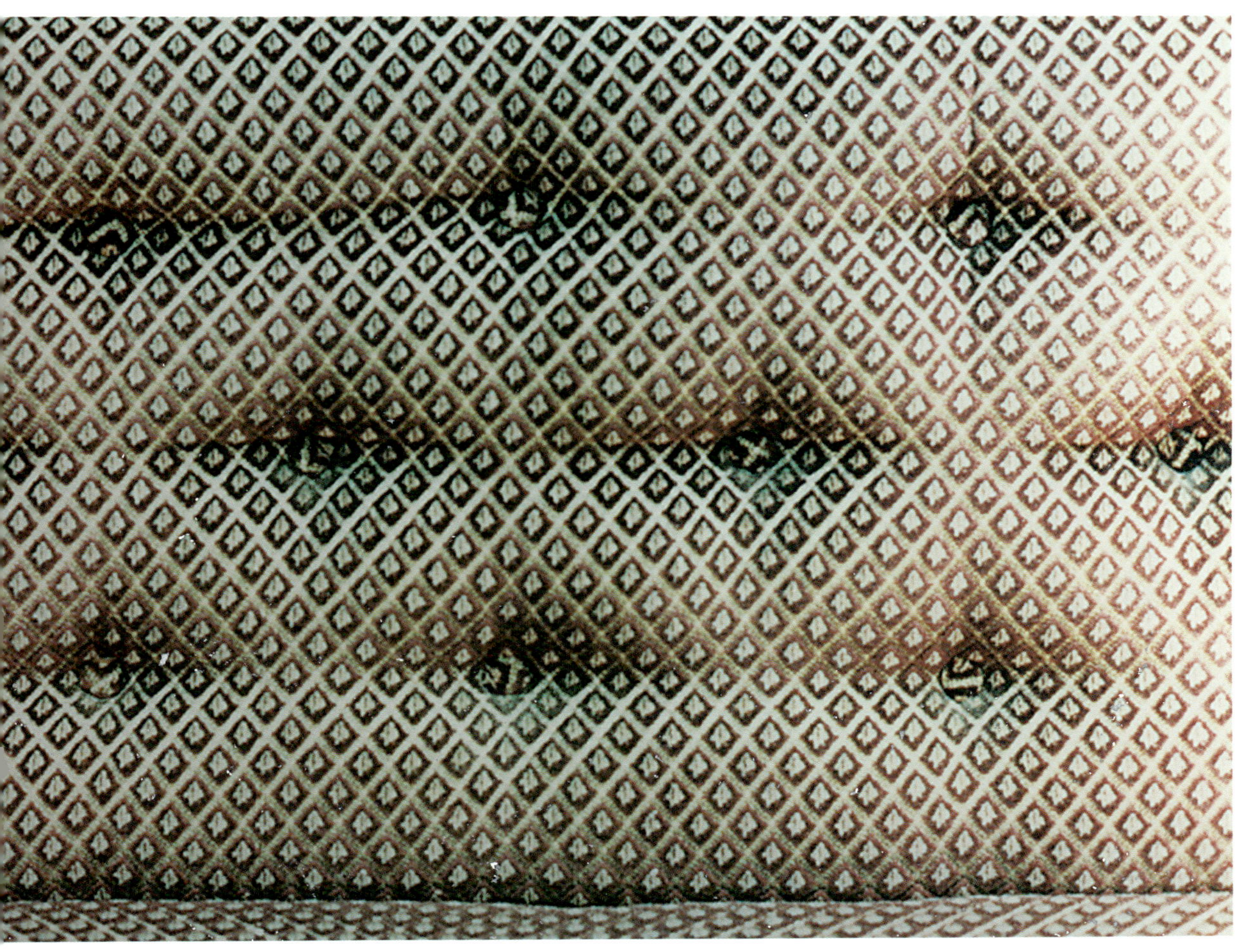

***cushion #1,* 2000**

c-print mounted to plexiglass

diptych: 60 x 40 x .5 inches each

air just occupies a larger ground and you
eshy belly button effect- it's more sensual.

– Joy Episalla

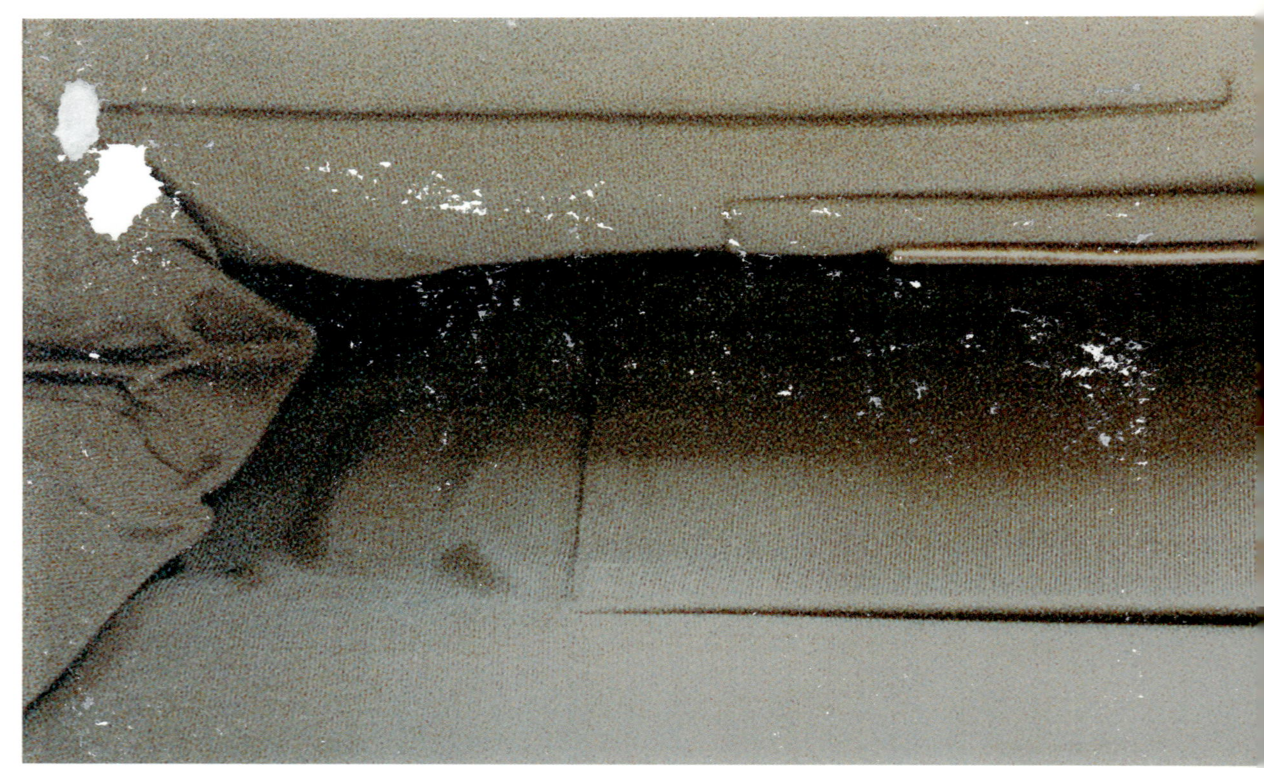

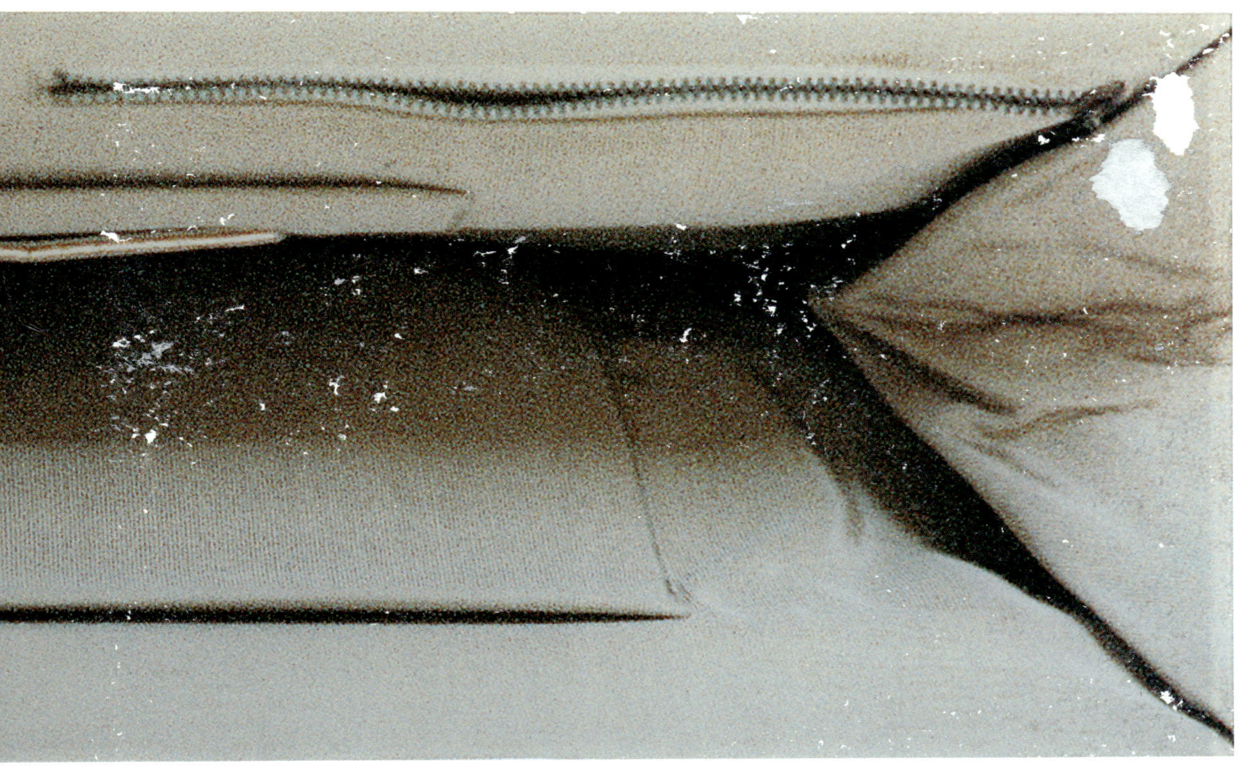

handbag #1, 1999

c-print mounted to plexiglass

56 x 16 x .5 inches

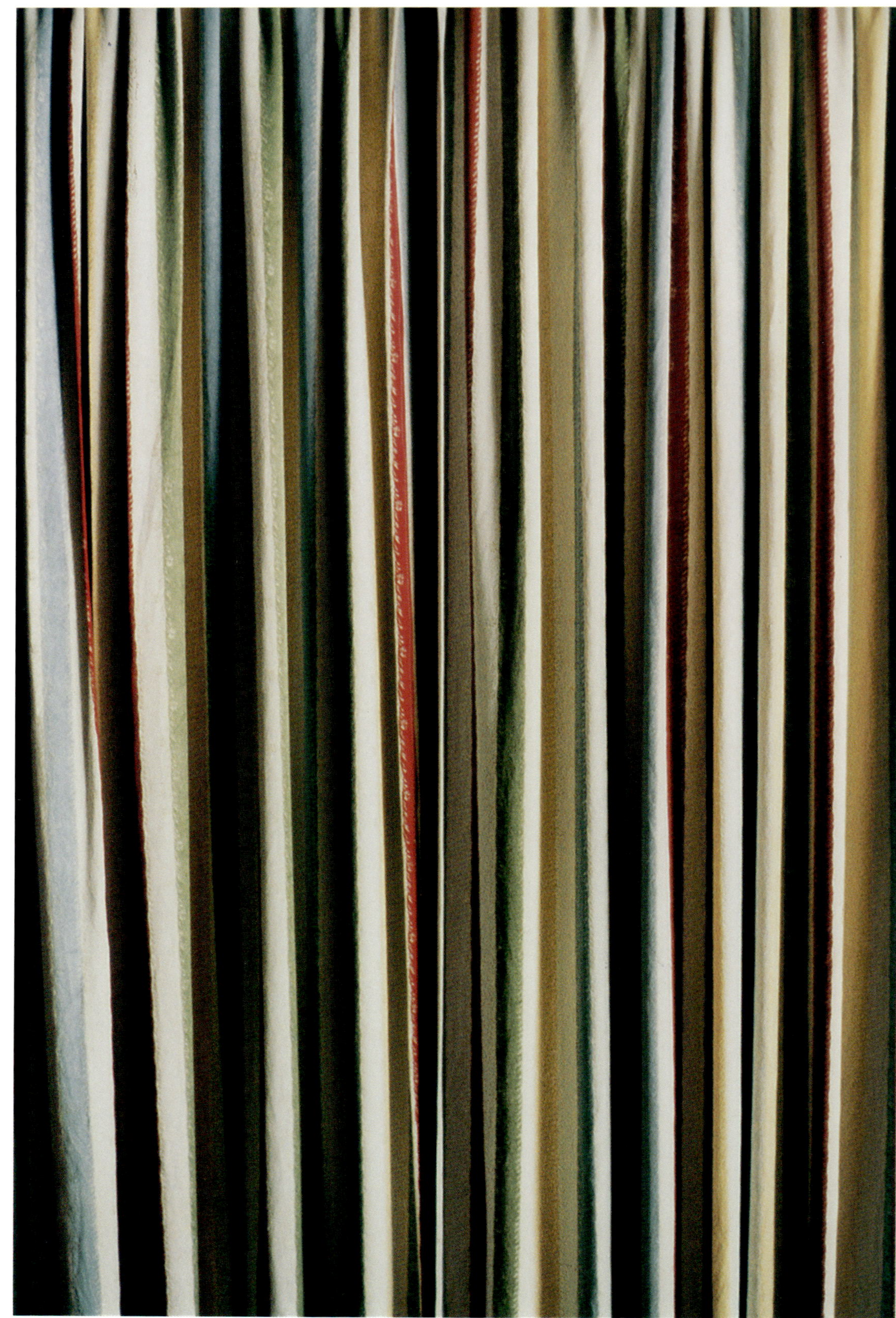

***curtain #20,* 1999**

c-print mounted to plexiglass

60 x 40 inches

Exhibition Checklist

curtain #20, 1999
c-print mounted to plexiglass
60 x 40 inches
courtesy of the artist and Debs & Co.

handbag #1, 1999
c-print mounted to plexiglass
56 x 16 x .5 inches
courtesy of the artist and Debs & Co.

cushion #1, 2000
c-print mounted to plexiglass
diptych: 60 x 40 x .5 inches each
courtesy of the artist and Debs & Co.

curtain #26, 2000
c-print mounted to plexiglass
40 x 30 inches
courtesy of the artist and Debs & Co.

cushion #2, 2000
c-print mounted to plexiglass
66 x 40 inches
courtesy of the artist and Debs & Co.

radiator #1, 2000
c-print mounted to plexiglass
5 panels: 26 x 39 x .5 inches each
courtesy of the artist and Debs & Co.

handbag #6, 2000
c-print mounted to plexiglass
34 x 32 x .5 inches
courtesy of the artist and Debs & Co.

pillow #2, 1999
c-print mounted to plexiglass
triptych: 40 x 60 x .5 inches each
courtesy of the artist and Debs & Co.

carpet #5, 2000
c-print mounted to plexiglass
36.5 x 58.5 x .5 inches
courtesy of the artist and Debs & Co.

carpet #3, 1999
c-print mounted to plexiglass
40 x 30 inches
courtesy of the artist and Debs & Co.

carpet #1, 1999
c-print mounted to plexiglass,
40 x 30 inches
courtesy of the artist and Debs & Co.

cushion #3, 2000
c-print mounted to plexiglass
60 x 40 x .5 inches
courtesy of the artist and Debs & Co.

Joy Episalla

	Born:	1957
	Lives:	New York City
Education	1979	BFA in Printmaking; California College of Arts and Crafts, Oakland, California
	1977-78	Attended Tyler School of Art; Rome, Italy
	1975-77	AA in Art and Design; Rochester Institute of Technology, Rochester, New York
Awards	1998	Braziers Workshop; Oxfordshire, United Kingdom
	1995	Braziers Workshop; Oxfordshire, United Kingdom
One Person Exhibitions	2000	"Joy Episalla, Recent Work," Clifford•Smith Gallery, Boston, Massachussets
	2000	"Joy Episalla," Mercer Union, Toronto, Canada
	1999	"inside/out," Debs & Co., New York, New York
	1998	Debs & Co., New York, New York
	1996	Neue Galerie/Interaktion Kunst; Hannover, Germany
Group Exhibitions	2000	"Meat Market Art Fair," Debs & Co., New York, New York
	2000	"Snapshot," The Contemporary Museum, Baltimore, Maryland
	2000	"Other Worlds," 28 Wooster Street, New York, New York
	1999	"Photic 2," eyewash, Brooklyn, New York
	1999	"Stars of Track & Field," Debs & Co., New York, New York
	1999	"Unbehagen der Geschlechter/ Gender Trouble; Neuer Aachener," Kunstrerein, Aachen, Germany
	1999	Starwood, Washington, DC
	1998	"New York Collection," Albright Knox Rental/Sales Gallery, Buffalo, New York
	1998	"Skin Deep," 123 Watts Gallery, New York, New York
	1998	"Brenner Pass/Liberty Exchange/Niemandsland, Part2," 4 Walls, Brooklyn, New York
	1997	100 Live Girls All Night, New York, New York
	1997	"Very Large Array," Debs & Co., New York, New York
	1997	"Brenner Pass/Liberty Exchange/ Niemandsland," 4 Walls, Italy/Germany
	1997	"Home is where the Heart is," White Columns, New York, New York
	1997	"Gramercy Art Fair," White Columns, New York, New York
	1997	"Silence = Death," Kunsthalle Dominikanerkirche, Osnabr̩ck, Germany
	1996	"Geopony," Adam Gallery, London, United Kingdom
	1996	"Graphic Responses to AIDS," Victoria & Albert Museum, London, United Kingdom
	1995	"interference," London Artforms Gallery, London, United Kingdom
	1995	"fruit x-x-x," Jacklight Gallery, New York, New York
	1995	"Other Rooms," Four Walls at Ronald Feldman Gallery, New York, New York
	1994	"Amendments," Hallwalls Contemporary Arts Center, Buffalo, New York
	1994	"Silence = Death," Deutsches Hygiene Museum, Dresden, Germany
	1994	"Before Stonewall," White Columns, New York, New York
	1993	"New Jersey Arts Annual," Newark Museum, New Jersey
	1993	"Contacts/Proofs," Jersey City Museum, New Jersey
	1992	"The Other Landscape," Tribeca 148 Gallery, New York, New York
	1992	"Urban Alchemy," OIA Gallery, New York, New York
	1991	"Outrageous Desire," Rutgers University, New Brunswick, New Jersey
	1991	"Situation," New Langton Arts, San Francisco, California
Articles	2000	"South End News, Episalla's Tower of Babel," Richard Foster, 19 October 2000, Vol.21, No.39, Boston, Massachussets
	2000	"Lesbian Art in America, A contemporary History," Harmony Hammond, Rizzoli International Publications, Inc., 2000, New York, New York
	2000	"eye, Recent Works," R. M. Vaughan, 16 March 16 2000, Toronto Canada
	2000	"The Globe and Mail, Gallery Going," Gillian MacKay, 11 March 2000, Toronto, Canada
	2000	"Art In America, Joy Episalla at Debs & Co.," Bill Arning, March 2000; New York, New York
	1999	"The New Yorker," Art / Galleries-Chelsea, October 4, 1999; New York, New York
	1999	"inside/out Joy Episalla," catalog with esaays by Linda Nochlin and Michael Cunninggham published by Debs & Co., September 1999, New York, New York
	1998	"Skin Deep," catalog, published by 123 Watts Gallery, 1998, New York, New York
	1998	"Wallpaper," an edition of 100 rolls of silkscreen wallpaper, published by Debs & Co., 1998, New York, New York
	1997	"Village Voice; Voice Choices," Kim Levin, 15 July 1997, New York, New York
	1997	"Joe Episalla,"catalog with text by Michael Cunningham, published by Neue Galerie, Hannover, Germany
	1996	"Lespress, ausgabe 10; jahrgang 2," October 1996, Frankfurt, Germany
	1996	"Third Text; Number 34," Spring 1996; London, United Kingdom
	1996	"Hannoveicche Allgemeine Leitung," 29 February 1996, Hannover, Germany
	1996	"Women's Art Magazine," January-February 1996; London, United Kingdom
	1995	"Time Out/London," 15-22 November 1995; London, United Kingdom
	1995	"The Times," *Art Review*, Sacha Craddock, October 1995, London, United Kingdom
	1995	"fruit x-x-x; Witness: An Exquisite Corpse," Summer 1995, New York, New York
	1994	"Silence = death; Kunst und AIDS in New York," 1994, catalog, Hannoversch AIDS Hilfe e.V., Germany
	•	member fierce pussy public art collective, 1991-95